SOCIAL AND ECONOMIC CHANGE IN

THE TRIBAL AREAS

1972—1976

The landscape of the Tribal Areas
(Tirah, Orakzai Agency)

SOCIAL AND ECONOMIC CHANGE IN

THE TRIBAL AREAS

1972—1976

By

AKBAR S. AHMED

FOREWORD

By

MAJOR-GENERAL (RTD.) NASIRULLAH KHAN BABAR

KARACHI
OXFORD UNIVERSITY PRESS
LONDON   NEW YORK   DELHI
1977

Oxford University Press

OXFORD LONDON GLASGOW NEW YORK
TORONTO MELBOURNE WELLINGTON CAPE TOWN
IBADAN NAIROBI DAR ES SALAAM LUSAKA ADDIS ABABA
KUALA LUMPUR SINGAPORE JAKARTA HONG KONG TOKYO
DELHI BOMBAY CALCUTTA MADRAS KARACHI

ISBN   0 19 577256 3

Printed in Pakistan by
Ferozsons Printers, Karachi.
Published by
Oxford University Press
P.O. Box 5093, Karachi, Pakistan

Foreword

In 1947, at the advent of Pakistan, the Quaid-e-Azam Mohammed Ali Jinnah in his sagacity and prophetic vision withdrew the armed forces from the cantonments around the Tribal Areas as a gesture of goodwill and a first measure towards integration. In the ensuing years the administration and the successive governments decided to leave the Tribal Areas to their own devices and only minimal social projects were undertaken. Thus, for 25 years, the Tribal Areas, 10,500 square miles in extent and with a population of 2.5 million were little more than a sociological curiosity.

With the advent of the People's Government, the Tribal Areas, too, began to be considered as within the pale of social and developmental activity. In his endeavour of assessment Prime Minister Z. A. Bhutto (then President) paid his first visit in 1972 and decided to embark upon a deliberate and massive developmental programme. What were till then considered the backwaters of Pakistan began gradually to enter the social and economic mainstream.

Mr. Bhutto's visit in November 1973 was of great significance. He dispensed with the traditional formal *jirgas* of elders and began a programme of addressing the people at large. This one single measure had a profound impact. The following three years saw unparalleled developmental activity: there was clamour from the public—more roads, more school, more hospitals, more electricity, more tube-wells—in fact, more of everything; there was an equal response from

the Government. November 1976 saw yet another
visit. The welcome was unprecedented in its enthusiasm.

The Prime Minister has thus triggered off events of
historical importance. The tribesmen now face the
future with confidence and a deep belief in their destiny,
a destiny that can have one and only one link—with
the Pakistani nation. In a remarkably short space of
time the Prime Minister has succeeded in welding a
people into a nation. The details of this achievement
are revealed for all to see in the pages that follow.

I was particularly pleased to learn that Mr. Akbar S.
Ahmed was writing this book. In the best traditions of
the Political Officers serving in the Tribal Areas he
combines his official interest in the tribes with serious
sociological and anthropological writings about them.
He is to be congratulated for not only projecting the
statistics of economic growth but also for relating them
so well to tribal social structure.

Major-General (Rtd.) Nasir Ullah Khan Babar
Governor, North West Frontier Province

Peshawar,
27 November 1976.

Contents

Contents

Plates

Maps

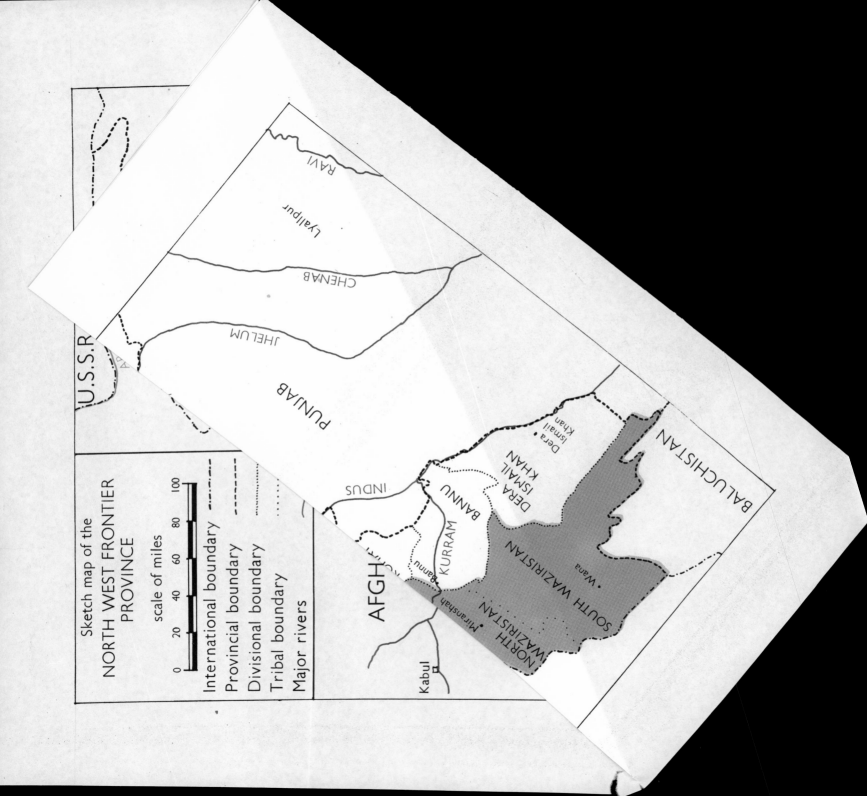

Sketch map of the
NORTH WEST FRONTIER
PROVINCE

scale of miles

0   20   40   60   80   100

International boundary
Provincial boundary
Divisional boundary
Tribal boundary
Major rivers

U.S.S.R.

RAVI

Lyallpur

CHENAB

JHELUM

PUNJAB

INDUS

BANNU

KURRAM

Bannu

Dera
Ismail
Khan

DERA
ISMAIL
KHAN

BALUCHISTAN

AFGH

Kabul

Miranshah

NORTH
WAZIRISTAN

SOUTH WAZIRISTAN

Wana

1

Introduction

The subject of this book is one of the most sensitive areas in Pakistan, and indeed South Asia, and has been the subject of great controversy, discussion and policy. However, we shall only be concerned with social and economic changes that are taking place in the Tribal Areas: political polemics are outside the scope of this book. These rapid changes in turn almost guarantee the passing of the traditional tribal way of life that has withstood the passing of many centuries. Economic de elopment, migration (to other cities in Pakistan and, of late, to the Gulf states) and education herald a new order. One of the key factors inhibiting economic development before the formation of Pakistan was the reluctance of the tribals to accept any development schemes from a government they considered foreign and alien. No such inhibition now exists.

Economic change in the Tribal Areas results in far-reaching changes in the tribal social structure. Where there is often intense democracy and intense cousin rivalry access to new avenues of wealth can elevate one individual or faction at the cost of the other. Today the tremendous development taking place in the Tribal Areas is creating new opportunities for the more vigorous and dynamic elements of society to emerge.

This essay relates the fundamental relationship in the Frontier between the social and economic lives of the tribe. Previous official studies have analyzed the subject from the point of view of political expedience or political solutions (as the term 'political' is understood in the Tribal Areas). Perhaps the main factor in understanding tribal social structure is that all aspects of human activity, whether social, economic or political, are interrelated. Once the tribal structure and its mechanics are clearly understood then policy-making at all levels of government becomes equally clear, and implementation of policy even more so.

This essay will review the major thrusts of economic development in the Tribal Areas from early 1972 to mid-1976. Economic activity on such a scale and at such a pace has previously been unknown in the Tribal Areas. Its impact on traditional social structure will be permanent. In tribal structures the opening of a road has important socio-political ramifications that may affect the social order. This essay will therefore examine economic statistics of growth and relate them to tribal social structure. After a period of intense activity this is a suitable moment to take stock and to examine the directions that lie ahead. It does not purport to make a statement on Frontier tribal policy or philosophy but merely sets out relevant facts: economic, sociological and administrative. Terms like Forward Policy, Modified Forward Policy or National Integration will be avoided as these clichés merely create barriers within countries. The developments in the last five years will be examined and assessed assuming that what has taken place is the inevitable march of a nation's progress and its attempts to bring its less developed regions on a par with its more developed regions.

1973-74 was the watershed period for the new tribal policy. Until then the old policies had regarded the Tribal Areas as a sort of 'special reserve' meant for Red Indian-type tribal species. It was in this period that the Prime Minister personally ordered the launching of a new tribal policy, the highlights of which were: the reactivation of the Razmak camp, the crossing of the Nahakki Pass, the shifting of the Mohmand Agency headquarters to Ghalanai and, in response to local requests, the creation of the new Orakzai and Bajaur Agencies. New colleges, roads and hospitals were granted and the major forts and posts that had become symptomatic of the general apathy towards tribal problems were vigorously reactivated and/or occupied. New possibilities were in the air. No place nor people was now too remote.

In addition to the very significant physical development of the last few years, a great impact has been made by the regular visits of the Prime Minister to the Tribal Areas. The force of this impact is evident when seen in the context of the old tribal political administration and social structure. The Prime Minister is the first head of government to visit every Political Agency in the Tribal Areas. He has not confined his visits to agency headquarters but often selected the more remote and peripheral places. The pattern of previous highly formal *jirgas* (assemblies) based on invitations to *maliks* (chiefs) in the Agency hierarchy was rejected. For the first time in the history of these areas open public meetings were held. There was no question of *khan* or non-*khan*, *malik* or non-*malik*, *mashar* (elder) or *kashar* (youth). Both the form and the content of the Prime Minister's speeches seemed to herald a new age for tribal people. The statistics of growth quoted in this book are a direct reflection of the personal interest of the Prime Minister in the Tribal Areas. The knowledge, policies and involvement of the one man ultimately, and in this case directly, responsible for the Tribal Areas may trigger changes that will permanently affect tribal social life. That this process has now begun, the reader may see for himself.

The social and economic changes in the Tribal Areas that we will be reviewing began in earnest in mid-1973. The present Governor of the North-West Frontier Province was then the Inspector-General, Frontier Corps, and in October 1973 he became the first official, along with the Political Agent, Mohmands, to cross the Nahakki Pass which had been closed since the 1935 campaign, and which had become a symbol of one of the final barriers to an adventure into the unknown. There was no road or even mule-track beyond Nahakki. I was privileged to be one of the first officials or outsiders to cross the Nahakki Pass shortly afterwards and drive with the Inspector-General up to Nawagai in Bajaur Agency and on the border of the Mohmand Agency. My own trips in the Mohmand area were connected with the selection of villages for a study in economic anthropology called 'the social organization of economic life among the Mohmand' sponsored by the Planning and Development Department of the N.W.F.P. Government.

I recall another trip a few months later again in the company of the Inspector-General and his answer to me when I remarked that the difference in the friendly reception the Safis were showing was nothing short of amazing. Brigadier (as he was then) Babar had said that the fundamental difference between the attitude of the tribesmen to the British and the Pakistanis was based on the fact that the latter were of the same stock and the same religion. Pakistan goes to the tribes with nothing to take but much to give, and both sides are now ready to enter into the relationship. This fact was quite evident from the difference in attitude I have mentioned above. Whereas many guns and groups were in evidence on my first trip the only pressure on us on subsequent trips was to stop and have tea or a meal. The Brigadier himself would disregard all protocol and humour the slightest whims of the tribesmen with patience and sympathy. He would drive his own jeep and stop for any hitch-hiker wanting a lift. 'This will get them used to travelling in vehicles and therefore on the Mohmand road' he would chuckle. I would like to thank him for his help, guidance and encouragement in the production of this book.

2

The North-West Frontier Province

The people and the area of the North-West Frontier Province are redolent of history and legend. Some of the most glamorous figures of history have been here. The list sounds almost incredible: Alexander, Taimur, Babar, Akbar, Ahmed Shah, and with the coming of the British, Napier, Nicholson, Churchill, Wavel and even Lawrence of Arabia. Generations of politicians, administrators and statesmen have been made or broken through their Frontier policies: Palmerston, Disraeli, Gladstone, Gandhi, Nehru and Mountbatten. Historically the forces that emanate from these areas have been of concern to Britain, India, Iran, Afghanistan, Russia and even China. On two occasions these forces have brought the world to the brink of war. The very names evoke strong feelings: tribal names like the Wazir, the Mahsud, the Afridi, the Mohmand. Or the names of places: Afridi Tirah, the most inaccessible area of the Tribal Areas; the Karakar Pass where in 1586 the Yusufzai annihilated an army of Akbar the Great Mughal; Saraghari, on the Samana range, where the Orakzais wiped out a Sikh detachment in 1897; in Waziristan, Ahnai Tangi where a British force was almost decimated with 2,000 killed or wounded including 43 officers killed; the dreaded Shahur Tangi where entire convoys have been trapped and wiped out; and, of course, the most famous Pass in the world, the Khyber.

Legend and romance have created a proto-type of the tribal surrounded by an indefinable air of mystery and high adventure. One of Kipling's most famous characters is Mahbub Ali who 'came from

that mysterious land beyond the Passes of the North'
(Kipling, 1960, p. 25). Even to the imperial Britisher
the tribal was a constant symbol of defiance and
cultural pride. I reproduce a paragraph that opens a
popular novel about the Frontier:

> Across the scrub-covered plain approached men with camels.
> The men had the faces of eagles and walked with along, slow,
> lifting stride. One of them looked up as he passed by. Anne
> smiled at him, expecting the salaam and the answering smile
> of an ordinary Indian wayfarer. But this was not India. The
> man stared her down, from pale green kohl-rimmed eyes.
> He carried a long rifle slung across his shoulders; a woman,
> shapelessly swathed in red and black cotton, swayed on top of
> the camel that he led; a lad of fourteen walked behind the camel;
> the lad had no beard, but his stride was an exact imitation of
> his father's insolent lilt, and he too carried a rifle.
>   'Pathans Aka Khel Afridis' Major Hayling said. Anne stared
> after them, a little angry, a little frightened. (Masters,1956, p.9)

The tribal way of life upholds its own severe code
extending beyond the limitations of both time and
space:

> Most of their grievances stem from *Zar*, *zan*, or *zamin*—gold,
> woman, or land. Vendettas may have their origins in trivial,
> even negative, action, such as a failure to show proper respect,
> but once begun they grow in size and violence; because a man
> has been slighted in a remote village by the Helmand river
> another may be murdered in Bombay or London or Paris many
> years later. Some vendettas are ended only after one of the
> families concerned has been wiped out, or has submitted to the
> ultimate humiliation of *nanawati* and throws itself at the feet
> of its enemy to ask for mercy. (Swinson, 1967, p. 20)

The Frontier way of life is tribal in the most profound
sense and its customs and traditions almost unchanged
for the last five centuries—certainly since the sixteenth
century when we hear from contemporary accounts,
like those of Babar, that most of the present geographical locations of the tribes were still the same then.

The Frontier problem and policy were tied to a
debate over two centuries as to the best possible
frontier line for the north west stretches of the
British Indian Empire. There were four such lines of
resistance:

Fort-like village in North Waziristan

Turi dance (Kurram Agency)

1. the natural geographical boundary provided by the River Indus,
2. the old Sikh line running between the foot-hills and the Settled Areas,
3. the so-called Scientific Frontier which drew a line between Kabul and Qandahar, and
4. the Durand line.

As we know, it was the last alternative that finally prevailed and which forms the present Pakistan – Afghanistan border. The selection of the last alternative was also a natural consequence of the Forward Policy. The Forward Policy culminated in and was partly the cause of the 1897–98 tribal wars along the Frontier. The arguments for the Forward Policy are clearly expressed in Bruce's book *The Forward Policy and its results* (Bruce, 1900). After these wars began what came to be known as the Close Border Policy, under which the tribes were to be confined to the Tribal Areas through a chain of posts and cantonments strung around the Tribal Areas. And this is how Pakistan found the situation in 1947.

The Tribal Areas are administered by the Governor of the N.W.F.P., as agent to the President representing the federal government, and today comprise seven political agencies: (north to south) Bajaur, Mohmand, Khyber, Orakzai, Kurram, North and South Waziristan. Malakand Agency (of which the states of Swat, Dir and Chitral were once part) is administered by the provincial government and is, therefore, technically not in the Tribal Areas which we shall be examining. We will concern ourselves with the seven agencies only.

Most of the agencies, including Malakand, were created late last century. In 1951 the Mohmand Agency was created from Peshawar District and in 1973 the two new agencies of Orakzai and Bajaur came into being. All the agencies, except Orakzai, have borders with Afghanistan along the Durand Line. A Political Agent heads the Administration of each agency. His role is discussed in a later chapter.

Apart from a Shia population among the Bangash and Turis in Kurram Agency and among the Orakzais, all Pathans are of the Sunni sect. The total population of the Tribal Areas in 1972 was 2,487,052 and the area is about 10,500 square miles. The annual income per capita is about Rs. 320 as compared to about Rs. 850 for the rest of the country. The average density of population is about 240 persons per square mile in comparison to 212 persons per square mile in the rest of Pakistan. The empty stretches and barren mountains may belie these figures but they include a substantial number of those members of the household who are working or living in the Settled Areas of the N.W.F.P., or in the other provinces or even abroad.

Perhaps the most significant political event in the history of this area took place when the Tribal Areas became part of the new state of Pakistan in 1947. Paradoxically, the two leaders of the new nation who best understood the psychology of the tribesman and his needs were not from this province at all. Both belonged to the province of Sind. Although there have been three heads of State who either belonged to the province, or largely served in it, it was left to these two to set in motion events with far-reaching beneficial social and economic ramifications.

The Quaid-i-Azam, Mohammad Ali Jinnah, had not only succeeded in establishing a personal rapport with the tribesmen, which was symbolized in his keeping the portfolio of the States and Frontier Regions himself, but made what, in retrospect, seems one of the most bold politico-military moves in history: immediately after the creation of Pakistan he ordered all troops posted in the formidable chain of forts that contained the tribesmen in the Tribal Areas along the tribal belt, to be vacated. Perhaps for the first time in recorded history there was no military barrier between the tribesmen and the towns of the settled districts. The citizens of Bannu could sleep peacefully at night without fear of Wazir raids and those of

Peshawar without the danger of Afridi raids. Over night camps like Razmak which once housed entire British army divisions became ghost-towns. The Quaid's brilliant strategic move paid off. The tribesman responded to this gesture by not only participating fully in the Kashmir battles that followed but also accepting the fact that as there were no alien or imperial masters to rule him he had no need for military fences to contain him and no cause to quarrel with the government. This signified his identity with a larger state.

Over the next two decades the tribesman came *down* to Pakistan but rarely did Pakistan *go up to* him. Then in 1973 Prime Minister Bhutto launched one of the most successful and spectacular economic programmes framed for a tribal people. Suddenly schools and dispensaries were being constructed in areas which could not boast a single cement building. Suddenly tractors and bulldozers worked in areas that had never seen even a bicycle. Suddenly roads were pushing their way through hitherto inaccessible areas and tribes. In their wake came light – literally, with the electric poles that followed the roads and metaphorically with the changing psychology of the tribesmen.

The high point of the present tribal policy was surely the reactivation of the Razmak camp which was carried out in the face of misgivings and many gloomy predictions by those who preferred the traditional policy of status quo. This was one of the most remarkable strategic moves in the Frontier in that it was conducted from start to finish without a single shot being fired, a clear enough indication that for the tribes such moves were a matter of government policy and not a threat to their structure or existence.

I reproduce two personal descriptions of Razmak to show what it once was during the British days and what it had become since:

Razmak, whence we had marched out on this column a few days earlier, was the largest of the garrisons in Tribal Territory. Here, on a plateau six thousand five hundred feet above sea level, secluded behind a triple circle of barbed wire and arc lights, had sprung up an unnatural town with a population of ten thousand men and three thousand mules. It bristled with guns, armoured cars, and all the panoply of war; but its inhabitants spent their time waiting for something to happen. (Masters, 1965, p. 15)

Professor Toynbee describes the same scene in 1960:

Picture to yourself Aldershot transplanted from England to Pakistan but retaining its English climate because it has been perched on a plateau 7,000 feet high, with mountains 10,000 feet high overhanging it. Then picture to yourself this expatriated Aldershot lying desolate and decaying. The decay is not yet far gone, because the place was built to last. It is built of solid masonry with corrugated-iron roofs. The church, the cinema, the shopping centre, the workshops, the officers quarters, the barracks: they are still well preserved; but the only building that is still occupied and used is the tehsil (the local administrative office). The avenues of trees still line the principal streets, but the roadways themselves are already half-overgrown with sumac bushes.

As a going concern, Razmak had a short life. (Toynbee, 1961, p. 152)

In August 1973 Razmak came to life again. Today it is the bustling headquarters of the Assistant Political Agent, North Waziristan, and the Scouts unit, the Shawal Rifles. Its future is assured. Plans are now afoot to open the first cadet college in the Tribal Areas. This prestigious college will be for tribal boys and will symbolize their growth and the pace of that growth.

3

Tribal social structure

THE TRIBE: THEORY AND REALITY

The application of sociological and anthropological knowledge to tribal administration is a well established fact in the social sciences. It is a fact that has often exposed anthropology to attacks from the Left as a tool of imperialism (Asad, 1973). Some of the greatest teaching anthropologists had once held administrative posts in tribal areas: Evans-Pritchard was Tribal Affairs Officer in Libya, an association which produced his classic, *The Sanusi of Cyrenaica* (1949) (its treatment of nationalist movements and its clearly anti-fascist sympathies show anthropology and imperialism need not go hand in hand), and Nadel who wrote *A Black Byzantium* (1942) and *The Nuba* (1947) was Secretary for Native Affairs in Eritrea.

Lord Hailey, himself a symbol of the link between tribal administration (in Africa) and professional anthropology, wrote in *African Survey* (1957): 'The professional anthropologist' should be 'of great assistance in providing Government with knowledge which must be the basis of administrative policy' (Asad, 1973, p. 85).

It is often claimed that the foundations of the subject were in part laid by civil servants working in British India. Sir Henry Maine, Law Member of the Viceroy's Council, wrote *Ancient Law* (1861) and *Village Communities in the East and the West* (1871) which are among the most significant early contributions. Sir Alfred Lyall, who was Agent to the Governor-General for the Rajput States and later Lieutenant

Governor of the North West Provinces for six years (whence Lyallpur got its name) wrote *Asiatic Studies: Religious and Social* (Tribal Series, 1882).

Although perhaps not academic in a technical anthropological sense Frontier studies, enriched by the work of soldiers and civil servants as a result of the first contacts between the British and the tribes, are a rich source of information for the ethnographer and the social scientist. Mountstuart Elphinstone wrote his vivid *An Account of the kingdom of Caubul* in the first years of the last century. This is the first English book on the Pathans and still remains one of the most accurate and interesting. Alexander Burnes wrote his *Cabool* just before his assassination in that city and on the eve of the First Afghan War. Herbert Edwardes wrote *A year on the Punjab Frontier 1848–49* on his experiences as the first Deputy Commissioner of Bannu (the college at Peshawar is named after him from the period when he was Commissioner of Peshawar). Warburton wrote *Eighteen years in the Khyber 1879–98* about his experiences of administering the famous pass and its tribes late last century. Colonel Pettigrew drew from his personal experiences with the Waziristan Scouts in *Frontier Scouts*. There are many more such examples.

The people of the North-West Frontier Province are not tribal in the sense understood in general sociological or anthropological literature. Primitive tribes are classified as: a) pre-industrial, b) pre-literate (Gluckman, 1971), c) speaking ancient or rare languages (like Dravidian), and d) being of aboriginal stock or not belonging to the main socio-cultural and ethnic groups (Bailey, 1961). In contrast to the last point Pathan tribes are part of what is called The Greate Tradition, that is part of or identifying with the universal and larger Islamic systems. Islamic norms, mores, customs and codes, originating from Arabia, are part of Pathan socio-religious and cultural behaviour.

Another major characteristic of primitive tribes is

economic backwardness coupled with a continuously widening gap in economic standards between the main socio-ethnic groups and the tribes. The aboriginal tribes of India are a good example:

> At the present rate of progress it will take at least fifty years more for the tribal people of India to catch up with the rest of the population as they are now. In the meanwhile 'the rest' will progress further at an even faster rate during the next fifty years. Thus the gap between the tribal and the non-tribals will widen even more. (Fuchs, 1974, p. 229)

The Frontier tribes, and specially their cousins in the settled areas, do not classify as tribes in this sense. They are literate and now moving towards advanced stages of economic and agricultural growth. Their competition with the more developed areas of the country leads one to the conclusion that their inherent dynamism will bring them to par within the next decade. This social and economic growth is an important characteristic of the Frontier tribes and in sharp contrast with tribes elsewhere.

The classical study on tribal societies still remains *African Political Systems* (Fortes and Evans-Pritchard 1970), although it was first published in 1940. The authors distinguished two forms of tribal societies: *Group A*, which consists of societies which have centralized authority, administrative machinery and judicial institutions supported by standing armies. They are stratified societies based on cleavages of wealth, privilege and status corresponding to power and authority. The Zulus of South Africa are a good example of this society.

Group B societies lack centralized authority, administrative machinery and constituted judicial institutions and there are no sharp divisions of rank, status or wealth. In spite of the absence of centralized institutions the society is far from chaotic in form and function and is referred to as 'ordered anarchy'. The Nuer in North-East Africa are a famous example of this type of society.

Although the above studies confine themselves to

tribes in Africa it is not difficult to place the Tribal Areas of the Frontier Province in this framework. From the view point of structural social anthropology the Frontier tribal societies provide exceptionally neat specimens of the segmentary principle in tribal society, that is the maintenance of political order over vast areas, no concentration of power or centralized authority, internal social cohesion and no stratification of aristocrats and commoners. Thus with minor exceptions, they belong to Group B. As we shall be examining the Tribal Areas within this framework it is essential that we take a closer look at the Group B societies. They have three major characteristics: the first and most important qualification is that the entire tribe traces its descent from one common male ancestor. He is the apical ancestor. For example the Yusufzai claim descent from Yusuf (*zai* is *zoi*, or *son*) or the Mohmands from Mohmand. Affiliated or attached clans, often in the form of occupational groups (like the blacksmith, barber or carpenter) that may not be actually related to the original ancestor, over time merge with the genealogical charter of the tribe and also call themselves after its main name. For example, the non-Mohmand barbers or blacksmiths living in the Mohmand area would call themselves Mohmand if asked their tribe. The household head or elder can trace his ancestry back to the founding father of the tribe. This 'generation recall' going back to seven or eight generations is in sharp contrast to the agricultural peasant societies where tracing of the genealogical charter to a known ancestor is of less significance and the greatest 'generation recall' is only four generations of ascendants (Mayer, 1970, p.170).

Secondly, these tribes are segmentary in composition: the entire body of society is made up of segments related to each other or, putting it in the traditional way, their genealogical lines resemble the branches of a tree that lead to the main trunk. For instance, the Mohmand tribe is divided into four major segments: the Tarakzai, Baezai, Khwaezai and Halimzai. Each segment is, in turn, divided into smaller segments. For instance the Halimzai is further sub-divided into Wali Beg, Hamza Khel and Kadi Khel. These segments are again sub-divided. The Wali Beg being divided on the basis of three brothers, Shati, Rasul and Maluk. The Shati, in turn, are divided into the descendants of two brothers, Ranra and Musa. This sub-division into increasingly diminishing segments takes on an almost geometrical pattern and enables each house in the tribal structure to trace its genealogy with accuracy and ease up to five or six generations. The Wali Beg, divided into its three major sub-segments, may be seen living today in the Shati Khel area in the Gandab: the Ranra Khel, the Musa Kor and the Maluk (or Sar Gul) Kor.

The following diagram, which has 'telescoped' certain unimportant lineages, will illustrate this branch-like aspect of Group B tribal society. In this diagram it is significant to note that the last line of the descendants of Mohmand are inter-related and (as it happens) alive:

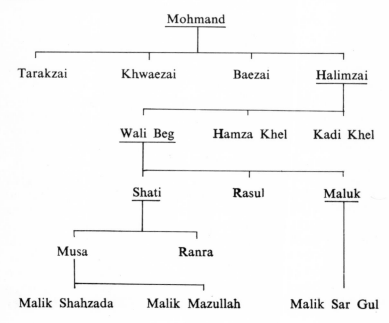

Putting it in another way, we may relate the conceptual segments of the tribe to the larger system of which they are part. The diagram below will illustrate the conceptual divisions of the Mohmand tribe by taking one example. If we look at the world through the eyes of Malik Shahzada this is the pattern of relationships that would emerge:

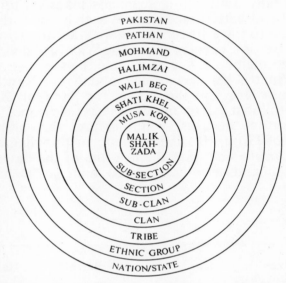

The third characteristic of these societies is that they are acephalous, (literally) without a head. Chiefs or leaders are largely confined to their own sub-segments (in our case the *kor*, or house) and very rarely, and then only on an individual basis, dominate the entire tribe. The concept of equality is so highly developed that many social scientists would prefer to call these tribal societies 'anarchic' as in *Tribes without Rulers* (Middleton and Tait, 1970).

Every household head is thus a 'petty chief' and no collective tribal action is possible without his consent. Joint action is determined by the tribal *jirga* which is the final expression of collective decision and action in Pathan society. One of the key economic factors that ensures socio-political equality is limited individual land ownership. The average holding of an entire house or family is one to three acres. It is a rare household with much more land. In theory this ensures the purest form of democracy in the world.

Part of Professor Barth's thesis (1959a and b) for the Swat Pathans appears to be applicable to the Tribal Areas: smaller groups do not exhibit tendencies towards 'fission' or 'fusion' in the face of larger opposing groups, as in African Group B societies, but tend to form part of a 'two-bloc system' that is represented at every level of tribal segmentation.

The tribal genealogical charter relates every member of society in one way or another, thereby creating kinship loyalties. These kinship loyalties in the Tribal Areas over-ride rational or bureaucratic considerations (a point clear to the Western anthropologist):

> In the developing countries bureaucratic rationality often loses out to kinship loyalties, an official selects his subordinates not on the criterion of ability to do the job, but on the basis of closeness of relationship. What to us is rank nepotism is to him a high moral duty. (Fox 1967, p. 14)

The emphasis in Pathan society on the role of male cousin, *tarboor*, (the father's brothers' son or as anthropological abbreviation puts it: fas brs son) is pervasive in all socio-economic dealings. 'Balanced opposition' in tribal structure means the opposing subgroups of cousins (fas brs sons), usually of that generation. There is a significant dividing line between true siblings and classificatory siblings. The answer to questions underlying both psychological and sociological motivation invariably lies in classificatory male kin or *tarboor* relationships. This highly competitive relationship and spirit often translates from political forms to agricultural or economic ones and might well be the driving force that has made, for example, the Mohmand name in the settled areas synonymous with hard working and conscientious agricultural tenants.

Economic activities, especially related to credit, are connected to the social structure which invariably focuses on kin (cousin) relationships. For instance it is seen how economic expenditure, borrowing and spending, for *rites de passage* is related to and translated from traditional father's brother's sons rivalry. Economic affluence, in turn, provokes and translates it into modern political rivalry. Credit seekers themselves might avoid father's brother's sons as sources of credit.

Economic life, with its peculiar situational constraints, is, then, related to the normative and cognitive values and structure of tribal social life. This now includes the impact of the modernization process on tribal structure and traditional social life.

The exceptions to the Pathan stateless societies are, of course, what were once the states of Dir and Swat. As these do not fall within the Tribal Areas under discussion we shall not concern ourselves with them.

A vital question in social surveys or essays is the extent and area of the universe under discussion. The tribals do not live in microcosmic, almost-complete, almost-isolable village units as does the population on the rest of the sub-continent (Bailey, 1960; Dube, 1965; Lewis, 1958; Mayer, 1970) or even in Pakistan (Ahmad, 1973; Alavi, 1971). They are organized in terms of segmented lineages which exhibit 'nesting attributes' typified, as we saw earlier, by Fortes and Evans-Pritchard as Group B tribal societies (1970). The segmentary descent system or the unilineal descent system is fundamental in identifying principles of social organization. Structural concepts may be applied from African Group A or B tribal types and those existing as 'ordered anarchies' (Middleton and Tait, 1970) when examining tribal structure, with the caveat that the crucial variable of an Islamic framework is important in considering any Pathan tribe.

Although tribal societies have been fairly well documented and studied there is a notable lack of socio-anthropological literature on Islamic tribes. What exists is, fortunately, of a high standard and of direct relevance and interest to a study of the tribes of Pakistan whether in the Frontier, Baluchistan or Sind Provinces: *Saints of the Atlas* (Gellner, 1969) is about the tribal Berbers of Morocco; the Cyrenaica tribes of Libya have been documented by Evans-Pritchard (1949) and Peters (1960); *The Kababish Arabs* (Asad, 1970) is about the Kababish in Sudan; *Social and Economic Organization of the Rowanduz Kurds* (Leach, 1940) and *Principles of social organization in Southern Kurdistan* (Barth, 1953) are about the Iraqi Kurds.

The Pathans have been the subject of many books of which the best known are probably *The Pathans* (Caroe, 1965), *The Pathan Borderland* (Spain, 1963), and *Afghanistan* (Fraser-Tytler, 1967). However, the first socio-anthropological studies of the Pathans and, incidentally, among the most brilliant theoretical contributions to the subject are Professor Fredrik Barth's studies of the Swat Pathans (Barth 1959a and b). Unfortunately, these rest on a fundamental flaw: they examine the society of Swat State in 1954 through the model of acephalous, segmentary, 'anarchic' structures. I have dealt with this in some detail in *Millennium and charisma among Pathans: a critical essay in Social Anthropology* (Ahmed, 1976).

Pathans identify themselves and maintain their ethnic boundaries through certain defined attributes:

1. *Patrilineal descent.* All Pathans have a common ancestor, who lived 20-30 generations ago according to accepted genealogies. . . . The acceptance of a strictly patrilineal descent criterion, however, is universal.
2. *Islam.* A Pathan must be an orthodox Moslem. The putative ancestor, Qais, lived at the time of the Prophet. He sought the Prophet out in Medina, embraced the faith, and was given the name of Abdur-Rashid. . . .
3. *Pathan custom.* Finally, a Pathan is a man who lives by a body of customs which is thought of as common and distinctive to all Pathans. (Barth, 1970, p. 119)

The significance of Pashto is not restricted to the language but forms attributes of cultural values which are beyond tribal or ethnic factors:

> The Pashto language may be included under this heading—
> it is a necessary and diacritical feature, but in itself not suffi-
> cient: we are not dealing simply with a linguistic group. Pathans
> have a explicit saying: 'He is Pathan who does Pashto not
> (merely) who speaks Pashto'; and 'doing' Pashto in this sense
> means living by a rather exacting code, in terms of which some
> Pashto speakers consistently fall short. (Barth, 1970, p. 119)

DEMOCRACY AND STRATIFICATION IN PATHAN TRIBES

So far we have considered the theory or the 'ideal-type' (which approximates closest to the ideal). Although societies in the Tribal Areas are largely segmentary and acephalous they may show variations in their socio-economic structure. My own findings are that detailed study will reveal that wherever the tribes have access to large tracts of fertile or irrigated land they tend to deviate from the democratic theoretical principles based on notions of *nang* (lit: honour) as the key symbol of society. I have considered this socio-economic analysis of sufficient importance to devote a full chapter to it, 'a theory of Pathan economic structure and political organization,' in my book (Ahmed, 1976). For instance, the landlords among the Yusufzai owned vast estates of irrigated lands and organized cultivation through tenants mainly from non-Yusufzai tribes. This social position was depicted accurately over a hundred and fifty years ago by Elphinstone (1972). Superior and inferior social positions were thus created. These positions in society were upheld and perpetuated through rents and *qalang* (lit: taxes) obtained from the tenants by the landlords. As *qalang* is the key factor in social interaction we may call this form of social organization *qalang* society and distinguish it from the other democratic form, which we may call *nang* society. The *qalang* phenomenon may also be found in the Tribal Areas. For instance in Orakzai Tirah, the Shia Pir families reinforced their religious hold over their Shia disciples by economic land holdings along the Mastura river.

The Shia Turi landed families did the same along the Kurram river in the Kurram Agency. The Khans of Nawagai and Khar, owning fertile land, in what is now Bajaur Agency, once held complete sway over their people. Bajaur provides the best example of the two opposing types of society living in one agency: the *qalang* ordered by the khans, and the Utman Khel, across the river, organized as a *nang* society. Apart from these 'deviations', Tribal Area societies approximate largely to the democratic segmentary and acephalous model.

The major differentiated and opposing economic, social and political attributes are listed below to illustrate the characteristics of the *nang* and *qalang* categories of Pathan social organizations suggested in this chapter:

THE 'NANG' CATEGORY	THE 'QALANG' CATEGORY
Economic	
1. hill areas	plain areas
2. largely unirrigated	largely irrigated
3. pastoral tribal economy	agricultural feudal economy
4. no rents or taxes	rents and taxes
Social	
5. mainly 'achieved' status of 'elders'	mainly 'ascribed' status of 'Khans'
6. illiterate, oral tradition	literate, orthodox, written tradition
7. acephalous tribal society organized in segmentary descent groups	autocephalous village organization under Khan
8. scarce population dispersed in 'fort-like' hamlets and nucleated settlements	dense population in large villages and tendency to urbanization
9. emphasis on *nangwali* (code of honour)	emphasis on *tarboorwali* (agnatic rivalry)
Political	
10. outside, or juxtaposed to, larger state systems	encapsulated within larger system; members of Civil Service, District Boards etc.
11. *jirga* represents interests of entire tribe (the vast majority of the population)	*jirga* members represent land-owners

12. warriors participating in   warlords organizing battles
    raids
13. egalitarian social organiza-   hierarchical social organiza-
    tion.   tion based on autochthonic
                                        population.

I hasten to qualify that these are merely symbols to differentiate and define two types of Pathan tribal structure and that *nang* values in themselves may be of equal importance in *qalang* societies (and even vice-versa).

A tribesman and his landscape

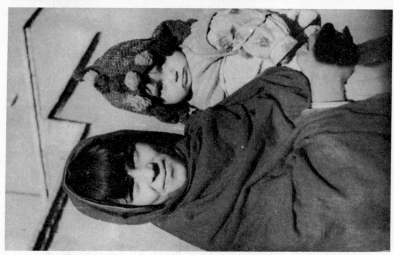

A mother and child   An elder
(North Waziristan)

4

The Tribal Agencies

The British first came into contact with the Frontier tribes when they defeated the Sikhs in 1849. At first there was no special agency for dealing with the tribal tracts and relations with the tribesmen were conducted by the Deputy Commissioners of the six districts (Hazara, Peshawar, Kohat, Bannu, Dera Ismail Khan and Dera Ghazi Khan). In 1876 the three northern districts formed the commissionership of Peshawar and the three southern ones that of the Derajat. In 1878, during the Second Afghan War, a special political officer was first appointed for the Khyber Agency. Kurram became an agency in 1892 and three years later the International boundary (popularly known as the Durand Line, after the head of the commission) was demarcated between Afghanistan and British India, and the need for a more definite tribal policy and administration became pressing. The Malakand and Waziristan Agencies were created in 1895-6. Malakand, at the outset, was placed under the direct control of the Government of India, all the other Agencies remaining with the Punjab Government until 1901 when Lord Curzon, Viceroy of India, created the North-West Frontier Province as a Chief Commissionership. Sir Harold Deane was appointed the first Chief Commissioner (the main hotel of Peshawar took its name from him). The tribal areas, however, came directly under the Central Government. Since that year only three new agencies have been created: the Mohmand in 1951, the Bajaur and Orakzai in 1973.

These agencies were often created with little sensitivity for ethnic configurations, and tribes that had been antipathetic to each other from time immemorial found themselves locked in the same Tribal Agency, as for example the Wazirs and the Mahsuds in South Waziristan. Worse still, certain tribes were cut by the international Durand Line into half, such as the Baezai and Khwaezai Mohmands.

The tribesmen themselves had a fair definition of their areas: *yagishtan* or 'land of rebellion' – echoing the 'orderly anarchy' concept of other such tribes elsewhere. More commonly, these areas were distinguished from the Settled Districts or *ilaqa* and called *ghair ilaqa* or 'outside the settled area'. Thus the Settled Districts became the pale and the Tribal Areas fell outside the pale. The special status and the ubiquitous evidence of guns confirms the above definition. However, I would like to draw a contemporary analogy to show that the social system and social life are not as irrational or anarchic as they may appear. The logic to acquire and carry guns is almost as sophisticated as the logic that enters nations in the nuclear arms race: you acquire the weapon so that it may act as a deterrent, more to show your opponent that you have one (and can use it) than actually to use it. The same principle works in the Tribal Areas and maintains a balance that deters anarchy or total breakdown of the system.

Islamic tribes have been analyzed in terms of 'nomadic' groups (Asad, 1970; Barth, 1961; Lewis, 1969; Tapper, 1971) or 'sedentary' groups (Barth, 1953; Gellner, 1969; Inayatullah and Shafi, 1964; Leach, 1940). We may attempt to analyze a third category: that of the *doa kora* tribal group. Let us look at the Mohmand Agency, a good example of the *nang* socio-economic category discussed in the last chapter. The Mohmands usually own two homes often at considerable distance from one another and are therefore called *doa kora* – 'those who own two houses'. Even so, the second home is spatially within the same sub-segment or group as the first one and either managed by close agnatic kin, brothers or sons, as joint property or owned outright in more affluent cases. It is important that the concept of *doa kora* is understood both in a literal and figurative sense. The *doa kora* category is as much a state of mind as a spatial or physical arrangement. All houses are of mud and the only valuable part is the wood-beam of the roof. They may thus be abandoned with ease. Life is spartan and possessions very limited. *Doa kora* therefore describes a critical aspect of the character and mental make-up of the tribesmen that affects socio-political behaviour. A man may cease to possess a house or land but cannot be deprived of his place in the tribal lineage charter. The tribals shift from one to the other house not like nomads in response to seasonal change but when and how the mood takes them or socio-economic compulsions dictate. Both houses are fully functional and interchangeable. Houses are also acquired or evacuated, especially in Tribal Areas, as a result of tribal feuds. Capturing a village or fort is one means of transferring property rights. The arena of interaction and conflict generally has fixed boundaries; for the Shati Khel Mohmand it is limited to the Gandab valley. The loser invariably shifts to the Settled Area and becomes one *kora* – but in his mind is the other *kor* lost in the Tribal Areas which he hopes to regain in his lifetime or that of his sons. This does happen frequently, as in the case of Malik L. in the Shati Khel area: (see diagram p. 26).

Though both houses may have a physical and lineage location, there is a constant tendency towards 'fission' as senior agnates break off to concentrate on one or the other house.

It is important that the identification with and emphasis on land, the earth (concept of Mother Earth and chthonic deities) in agricultural peasant societies is not found in the Tribal Areas. Emphasis in the Tribal Areas is on descent groups and filiation in the lineage structures. One may lose land in Shati and

CYCLICAL INTER-GENERATIONAL FORTUNES OF MALIK L

1. ML's father expelled by cousins from Tribal Areas to Settled Areas.

2. Family makes fortune as agricultural tenants in Settled Areas. Eldest son born.

3. ML returns to Tribal Areas aided by local factions and claims land based on position in tribal charter.

4. ML reinforces political position in Tribal Areas with economic position based on fertile land in Settled Areas and is recognized as 'Malik'. Elder son sists for B. A. and applies for Commission in the Army: he symbolizes new economic and political status and strength of ML.

be ousted from the Tribal Areas but one retains ones position and rights in the tribal charter.

Names of villages are specifically based on the most senior living agnate in Tribal Areas, for example, *Malik Shahzada Kilay*, 'the village of Malik Shahzada', the senior member of the *Musa Kor*. They may also be named after the sub-group of the segment, for example, Ranra Khel. Villages may even have temporary and dual names. Ranra village is also known by the name of its senior living malik, Mazullah Khan. Shati is named after the segment of the Halimzai clan, Shati Khel. Its name has no other geographical or historical association. Tribal Area villages are small and contain sub-segments invariably descended from a ccmmon senior male agnate. The entire population may consist of an elementary, nuclear family (ML's village) or a compound family if the senior is a polygynist (Shahzada Malik village). The total population living within the fort-like compound would be between 20 to 80 people. Larger villages with populations ranging from 150 to 200 are inhabited by several married brothers living clustered together as a joint family as in Sar Gul village.

Tribal society is patrilineal and democratic in a manner that is pregnant with consequences for the lives of its members. After marriage the bride usually comes to live with the husband, it being rare for the groom to go to live with the bride except in cases where blood feuds may prompt migration. This custom, called 'virilocality' in anthropological literature, in itself underlines the nature of Pathan society which reckons descent only through the male line. Succession, whether through brother or father, is always and only through the male line. There is a high incidence of *badal* (literally *change* and not here used for 'revenge') marriages in which a sister or cousin may be given in marriage in exchange for the marriage of the other person's sister or cousin. For example, if A marries B's sister, B marries A's sister as *badal*. These marriages do not involve either the exchange of bridal gifts or bride-wealth.

It is worthwhile noting that no concepts of ritual purity or impurity segregate Pathan tribesmen in commensal or social habits. There is marked traditional respect for the elder ('white-beard') or malik but all tribesmen sit and eat together from the same table-cloth and even the same plates.

The role of water must be emphasized in tribal lives: scarcity of it in the Tribal Areas and often, paradoxically, an excess of it in the form of floods, in the Settled Areas. Tribal strategy in feud and conflict is based on capturing the well or water tank of the opponents. The ethno-demography of the housing patterns in the Tribal Areas often relates directly to the strategy of tribal warfare and access to the water well or spot.

Social analysis of the Tribal Areas is generally made in terms of lineage segments (*khels*) corresponding to marked territorial divisions while that of Settled Areas in terms familiar in literature dealing with village boundaries and units. For instance, the barber (*nai*) does not live in the Shati area but visits in a week the entire sub-segment of the lineage covering a couple of square miles. He is paid traditionally in kind whereas in the Settled Area he lives and works largely in the village itself, although he may still take traditional payment in kind after every crop. Consequently we have to discard the notion of a village as a unit of study in the Tribal Areas.

Four of the seven Tribal Agencies are named after the dominant tribe of the agency (Mohmand, Orakzai, North and South Waziristan) and three after geographical areas or features (Bajaur after the area, Khyber after the Pass and Kurram after the river). The Tribal Areas differ vastly in scenery and geography, but there is always a back-ground panorama that is as compelling as the people who live in these areas. The stretches of shrub and dwarf-palm in the valleys, the power of the fast mountain streams and rivers, the immediate presence of towering heights or the bold sweep of vast plains, present a picture of the magnificence and majesty of nature that is difficult to equal anywhere in the world.

> One secret of the hold of the North-West Frontier is to be sought in the tremendous scenic canvas against which the Pathan plays out his life, a canvas brought into vivid relief by sharp, cruel changes of climate. Sometimes the assault on the spirit is that of stark ugliness and discomfort—appalling heat, a dust-storm across the Peshawar plain, the eroded foot-hills of Khaiber or Waziristan; more often it is an impression of beauty indescribable in its clarity and contrast with the barren emptiness that went before. The waft and warp of this tapestry is woven into the souls and bodies of the men who move before it. Much is harsh, but all is drawn in strong tones that catch the breath, and at times brings tears, almost of pain. (Caroe, 1965, p. xiii)

This background relief contrasts sharply with and even underlines the nature of tribal demography. The tiny villages remain spread far and wide bearing testimony to the tribal system and the desire to live independently rather than in clusters and townships—a characteristic of *nang* social systems. It is a sociological fact of immense significance, that almost explains the tribal character, that there are no (nor have been) great cities or indigenous towns in the Tribal Areas. The growth of the present focal points of trade and commerce, such as Wana in South Waziristan or Parachinar in Kurram, began with the coming of the British and the creation of the Agency headquarters.

In the following pages we will glance briefly at each Agency in turn. Figures are based on the latest Pakistan population census conducted in 1972.

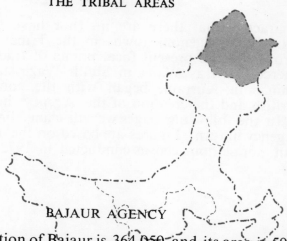

BAJAUR AGENCY

The population of Bajaur is 364,050 and its area is 590 square miles. The main tribes are Utman Khel and Tarkani of which the major sections are Mamund and Salar Zai. Churchill campaigned here (and in the Mohmand areas) in the last years of the last century and wrote of his adventures in 1898 in *The Story of the Malakand Field Force* (1972). It was created as an Agency from a remote subdivision of the Malakand Agency on 1 December 1973 with Headquarters at Khar. Before 1960 Bajaur was treated as an almost wholly inaccessible area and it was in that year that an Assistant Political Agent was appointed whose headquarters, however, were outside the agency at Munda, in Dir District.

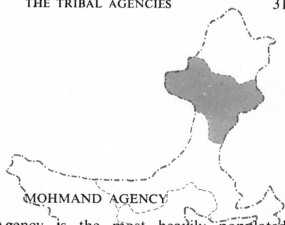

MOHMAND AGENCY

Mohmand Agency is the most heavily populated Agency with a population of 382,922 and an area of 887 square miles of territory. The Agency was created in 1951 before which the Mohmand tribes were administered by the Deputy Commissioner, Peshawar. Apart from the Mohmand tribe the agency contains the Safis who, because of their association with the Mohmand, are often called Safi Mohmand. Until 1973 the headquarters of the Mohmand Agency were in Peshawar when they were moved to Ekkagund. This year the thrust has been completed and the permanent agency headquarters are almost complete at Ghalanai, deep in the Mohmand Agency. There is scant rainfall and little irrigated land, a factor responsible for the large demographic movements of the Mohmands to the fertile lands of Charsadda and Mardan.

KHYBER AGENCY

The Khyber Agency has a population of 377,001 and an area of 991 square miles. The majority of the tribes in this agency are Afridis, of which there are eight major sections. However, there are important pockets of Mullagoris, (Mohmand) Shilmanis, and Shinwaris, the last around and in Landi Kotal on the Pakistan – Afghanistan border. The Afridis are famed as the tribe that controls the Khyber Pass and also as the inhabitants of what is still one of the most inaccessible areas, Afridi Tirah. This strategic situation has enabled the Afridis to force every conqueror in history passing through the Khyber to come to terms with them. They have a formidable battle record for strategy and tenacity in the mountains. They once annihilated an entire Mughal army of Aurangzeb's.

The agency headquarters are in Peshawar in winter when the tribes migrate to the comparatively warmer Khajuri plains just beyond the Bara market town (five miles from Peshawar). New water schemes on the Bara river are converting the semi-arid and barren Khajuri plains into valuable land for cultivation and habitation. Brick houses are appearing at a rapid rate. The summer headquarters are in Landi Kotal on the international border. Jamrud, (deriving its name from the Iranian Emperor Jamshed who ruled here some 2,000 years ago) sits at the mouth of the Khyber Pass about ten miles from Peshawar. A Sikh fort that looks remarkably like a battleship still dominates the Jamrud area. The Kuki Khel Afridis live here. Shagai fort, ten miles from Jamrud, with its squash courts and swimming pool, is one of the best maintained and striking on the Frontier. Ali Masjid (Hazrat Ali, the son-in-law of the Holy Prophet is said to have prayed here) is the highest point and key to the Pass.

The Pass itself is about 25 miles long. The Tahtarra range dominates the entire pass and is clearly visible from Peshawar and its environs. The first Political Officer was Major Cavagnari, appointed in 1879, and the first Political Agent, Major G. Roos Keppell (1902).

ORAKZAI AGENCY

Orakzai Agency has a population of 278,951 and an area of almost 700 square miles. The Orakzai tribes take their name, which literally means 'the lost son' (*orak zoi*), from a romantic legend about their ancestor, Sikander Shah, a Prince from Iran. The Prince was exiled or 'lost' and after many adventures married and ruled in Tirah. The four major non-Orakzai tribes, the Ali Khel, Mullah Khel, Mishti and Sheikhan are now for all purposes like the other Orakzai tribes. Certain Orakzai tribes, like the Masozai and half the Lashkarzai (the other half, the Mamozai, inhabit the Khanki river valley in the Agency) find themselves in Kurram Agency for historical and administrative reasons. A small Bangash tribe, the Biland Khel, is attached to the Orakzai Agency also for administrative and historical reasons, although they lie at some distance from the Agency between Thal and North Waziristan (by the entrance to the Spin Wam – Mir Ali road). Over one-tenth of the entire population of the agency is of the Shia sect. The Shia areas in Tirah receive heavy rainfall and especially along the Mastura river (which divides them from the Sunni Daulatzai) fine wheat, maize and rice crops are grown.

The Prime Minister had announced the creation of the agency at a Grand Tribal Jirga at Samana and it began functioning on 1 December 1973. Before this date the Orakzai tribes were part of Kohat and Hangu Frontier Regions. The headquarters of the agency are temporarily at Hangu, in Kohat District, but land has been acquired in Orakzai Tirah for the agency headquarters, in the Kalaya valley and by the Mastura. The valley is flanked by mountain ranges between 6,000 to 7,000 feet high.

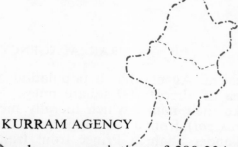

KURRAM AGENCY

The Kurram Agency has a population of 280,234 and an area of 1,305 square miles with its headquarters at Parachinar. It was occupied in 1892 by the British at the invitation of the Turi Shia tribe who feared aggression by the neighbouring Sunni tribes. Half the agency was called the Administered Area, mainly along the Kurram River valley, and the other half the Frontier Regions. The Administered Areas are mostly inhabited by Turi and Bangash Shias and contain fine cultivated lands. The waters from the Kurram feed lush green paddy plots. The Frontier Regions, in contrast, remained closed until 1974 and as a result the Para Chamkani, Massozai, Ali Sherzai and Zai Musht, totalling just over half of the agency population, have lagged behind in development. The first Political Agent, W.R.H. Merk, was appointed in 1892.

Because of its semi-settled history Kurram has attracted more tourists than any other agency. Parachinar (5,931 feet above sea level) is delightfully situated and the snow-covered mountains above it provide a scenic setting of great splendour. It is approached by a good motorable road that runs parallel to the Kurram river. Parachinar has grown into a bustling little market town.

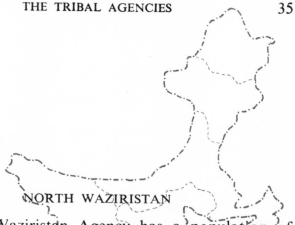

NORTH WAZIRISTAN

The North Waziristan Agency has a population of 250,663 of which the Wazir tribes account for about 160,000. It covers an area of 1,817 square miles. Both Mahsuds, entirely in South Waziristan, and Wazirs are Darwesh Khels. The North Waziristan Wazirs are Utmanzai of which the major sections are Wali Khel, Momit Khel and Ibrahim Khel. Some 50,000 Daurs constitute an important minor tribe of the Agency and are said to be the original inhabitants. The headquarters are at Miran Shah. Major C.A. Smith was the first Political Agent in 1910. North and South Waziristan have been the scene of fierce battles with the British and the legendary Faqir of Ipi, Mirza Ali Khan, a Tori Khel Wazir, conducted his major encounters with the British in this region. His headquarters in the caves of Gurwekht gained international fame.

SOUTH WAZIRISTAN

The South Waziristan Agency has a population of 307,514 and an area of 2,556 square miles. Three-quarters of the population are Mahsud, the remaining quarter, Wazir. This division based on the traditional *nikkat* (ancestral hereditaments) was confirmed by the British as the basis for all tribal dealings whether in terms of profit or loss, reward or punishment. Wana, the summer headquarters of the Political Agent, is situated in the Wana plain which is some thirty miles long and ten miles broad, and the home of the Ahmad Zai Wazirs. The winter headquarters of the agency are at Tank, in Dera Ismail Khan District, which is mostly owned by Mahsuds, who filled the vacuum left by Hindu migrants in 1947.

Deep in Mahsud territory is the centre of the Urmars at Kaniguram. The Urmars are believed to be the aboriginal people of this area and have a pre-Islamic past. Their language derives from Sanskrit although they are Pashto-speaking today. Kaniguram is famous historically as the place that gave birth to the Ro-shania movement during the Mughal era in the six-teenth century. Pir Roshan, ('saint of light', or as his opponents called him Pir Tarik: 'saint of darkness') is buried near Kaniguram. The housing pattern of Kaniguram is distinct from other typical tribal villages as the houses are placed together, indeed almost on one another, and the large village is dense and crowded. The daggers of Kaniguram are famous for their craftsmanship.

FRONTIER REGIONS

Apart from the above agencies there are comparatively smaller tribal pockets called Frontier Regions
(F.Rs.) attached to various Districts and administered
by the Deputy Commissioner. For instance, the
Bhittani and Sherani of F.R. Dera Ismail Khan are
with the Deputy Commissioner, Dera Ismail Khan,
and the Bhittanis and Wazirs of F.R. Bannu with the
Deputy Commissioner, Bannu. The Deputy Commissioner, Kohat, has the Darra Adam Khel Afridis in
his charge. Darra Adam Khel has gained an international fame, or notoriety, over the last hundred
years, for its 'arms factories'. Tribals manage and own
little workshops here producing a superb variety of
imitations of the most sophisticated and best in gun-
nery. The population and area of the F.Rs. is given
below:

	Population	Area (in square miles)
Peshawar F.R.	60,132	191
Kohat F.R.	38,238	163
Bannu F.R.	63,882	339
D. I. Khan F.R.	76,472	1,247

A *naik* and his Sikh protégé (Orakzai Tirah)

A *naik* and his Hindu protégé (Orakzai Tirah)

5

Tribal Institutions

Some useful words that signify individual or collective tribal functions are given below. These words are common to Pathan society and language but some, for obvious reasons, have fallen into disuse in the Settled Areas. The first four institutions form the major components of *Pukhtunwali* or 'the way of the Pathans' but the following in one way or another also relate to it:

1. *melmastia:* The first law of the *Pukhtunwali*. This means the showing of hospitality to all visitors without hope of remuneration or favour.

2. *badal* (literally: *revenge*). The second law of the *Pukhtunwali* means the taking of revenge over time or over space to avenge a wrong.

3. *nanawatay* derives from the verb to *go in* and is used when the vanquished party is prepared to go in to the house or *hujra* of the victors and beg forgiveness. There is no *nanawatay* when the dispute involves *tor* (*see* 5 below) or injury to women.

4. *nang* (literally: *honour*) is composed of the various points below that a tribesman must observe to ensure his honour, and that of his family, is upheld.

5. *tor* (literally: *black*) relates to those cases that are concerned with the honour of women. *Tor* can only be converted to *spin* (*white*) by death.

6. *tarboor* (literally: *cousin*). In tribal society the *tarboor* or father's brother's son has a connotation of agnatic or cousin rivalry and enmity.

7. *lashkar* is the tribal army. It implements the decisions of the *jirga*.

8. *jirga* is an assembly of tribal elders called for various purposes whether waging war or composing peace, tribal or inter-tribal.

9. *chalweshti* derives from the number forty and means the tribal force that would implement the decision of the *jirga*. Every fortieth man of the sub-section would be a member. In Kurram this force is called *shalgoon* which derives from the number twenty and means that every twentieth member will be part of the force.

10. *teega* or *kanrai* (lit: *stone*) means a fixed date until which all hostilities between warring factions will be suspended. The tribe then ensures the implementation of the *teega*. There is an interesting theory that this custom derives from a pre-Islamic Rajput practice of writing an agreement on a stone and placing it at a place selected by the tribe (King, 1900, p. 49).

11. *nikkat* derives from the noun *nikka* which means grandfather. In the Tribal Areas *nikkat* means the specific distribution of profit and loss that each tribe and sub-tribe has to bear. It thus takes on the meaning of hereditary rights and obligations, or hereditaments. This distribution is not based on current population figures but was fixed some generations ago and may therefore appear unbalanced and unfair in the light of the present population.

12. *badragga* means a tribal escort usually composed of members of that tribe through which the travellers are passing. If a *badragga* is violated a tribal feud will follow.

13. *hamsaya* is a word used for client or dependent groups who attach themselves to larger or stronger maliks. The protector of non-Muslim groups (like Hindus and Sikhs) is called a *naik* in Tirah. Any attack on a *hamsaya* is considered as an attack on the 'protector'.

14. *qalang* (lit: *rent* or *tax*) is taken by a landlord from his tenants. It is in this context that I have used the word, which is common among the Yusufzai, although there may be other meanings attached to it elsewhere.

15. *malatar* means literally *tying the back* and refers to those members of the group who will actually join the fighting on behalf of their leaders or with him.

16. *muajib* means the yearly (or half-yearly) fixed allowances paid by the political authorities to the tribe and its various sections.

17. *lungi* means the allowances given. by the political authorities to individual maliks.

18. *nagha* is a tribal fine decided by the council of elders and imposed upon the wrongdoer. It is extracted, if necessary, by force (i.e. the mobilization of a *lashkar*) and the wrongdoer may have his house burned.

19. *rogha* means settlement of a dispute between warring factions.

20. *hujra* is a common sitting (or sleeping) place for males in the village. Visitors and unmarried young men sleep in the *hujra*. Expenses are usually shared by the village. Almost every *hujra* has a mosque adjacent to it in the village structure.

6

The role of the Political Agent

The role of the Political Agent has been described as 'half-ambassador and half-governor' (Spain, 1972, p. 24). He administers his agency on behalf of the government with a necessary mixture of tact, patience, wit and sympathy. The sympathy of the Political Agent for his tribes is proverbial and many amusing anecdotes are told. I repeat one that illustrates this identification with the tribe:

> There was a tale current in the folklore of Indian clubs and messes for which there was perhaps no historical authority but which did enshrine a truth. It concerned a Political Agent accompanying troops on a punitive expedition. After breakfast with the officers, he took his lunch in a haversack and disappeared; they did not see him again till evening when, sipping a pink gin by the light of a lantern carefully screened from snipers, he asked: 'And how did things go on your side today? Casualties on our side were half-a-dozen. (Woodruff, 1963, p. 153)

Sometimes he waves the flag, present in the shape of the Frontier Corps and its famed Frontier Scouts. The Scouts, apart from the *khassadars*, the local tribal force, are his only police force. In the absence of a popular political representation his powers and prestige are great and in his person he represents the government itself.

Once members of the elite Indian Political Service (of which two-thirds were from the army and one third from the Indian Civil Service) manned the agencies. The power, prestige and glamour of the Political Agent's job was unrivalled on the subcontinent.

The regular criminal, civil and revenue laws do not apply in the Tribal Areas and the tribes conduct their affairs through their own set of codes, the *Pukhtun-wali* (described in the previous chapter). It is only on the main roads and in the agency headquarters that the Political Agent can take action against criminal behaviour under the Frontier Crimes Regulation. However, the political officers ensure that no inter-tribal conflict, however remote, gets out of hand and that no law and order problem assumes uncontrollable proportions. A great deal of the administration depends on the Political Agent's personality and relations with the tribes and their leaders.

Before Partition the British Political Agents often faced the wrath of the tribesmen as the focus of the imperial power. Waziristan has a record for murdered Political Agents and officers. One, Bowring, was killed by his orderly for sleeping with his feet towards *Kaaba Sharif*. Major Dodd, another Political Agent, South Waziristan, was shot by his own orderly with a weapon that he had given to the assassin as a present. The legendary Colonel Harman, who raised the South Waziristan Militia, was bayoneted in the Wana mess.

The emphasis in the Political Agent's role is shifting from that of upholder of the status quo to the main force behind development and change. He is also the Project Director of the Rural Works Programme and, as the person responsible to Government for the tribes, he is often involved in the dealings of almost all departments. For instance, the Public Works Department Engineer might find his work on a road hampered by a recalcitrant malik in which case he will appeal to the Political Agent to use his influence in removing the obstacle.

A typical agency administrative chart may look something like this:

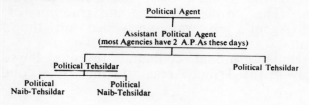

This, in fact, is the present administrative arrangement of the Orakzai Agency. Each Political Tehsildar/ Naib-Tehsildar is in charge of distinct tribes. As tribes in the Tribal Areas live within specific boundaries that correspond to geographical or physical areas the Agency is divided both by tribe and area for purposes of administration.

As education filters through and its advantages become apparent the tribes themselves approach the Political Agent for new development schemes. For instance, in 1973 in the newly-opened areas of the Safi Mohmands most tribesmen were reluctant to accept schools and dispensaries as they felt this would involve a loss of their independent status. Today the same tribesmen visit the Political Agent, Mohmands, or the Governor's House in Peshawar clamouring for more development schemes and expenditure.

Formerly a single Political Agent with little to do except 'contain' his tribes and maintain the status quo could control his agency with ease. Today various pressures on him, through increasing education, development demands and the 'sedentarization' process of the tribesmen in the Settled Areas, almost predict the day he will either have to share his responsibilities with local tribal advisory councils or delegate some of his powers and duties for them to be performed satisfactorily.

7

Leadership groups

THE MALIK AND THE MULLAH

Pure tribal structure does not admit hereditary rights of leadership and socio-political division between superior and inferior status. The *malik* (from the Arabic for *king*) represents traditional tribal leadership based on respect for age and, where evident in individual cases, the other qualities of leadership, like wisdom, generosity and bravery—virtues highly respected in Pathan society. In the tribal areas it is still a common saying that 'every man is a malik unto himself'. The *mashar – kashar* (*elder – youth*) conflict that has taken various quasi-political shapes these days is another aspect of this problem. Although it is underlined that this is not a generation clash and that *kashar* in this context does not imply *young* or *youth* as much as *have-nots* in the face of the elder *haves*.

To the average tribesman the maliki system, within the framework of tribal administration which traditionally patronizes selected and favoured maliks, is an institution foisted on him by the British for their own political and administrative purposes. The malik in pure tribal structure rarely represents more than the immediate interests of his joint family or subsection. His social role within his tribal structure and for his subsection is beneficial and often represents good sense and influence. He is the major living link in the section's genealogical chain that ties the individual to the founding father of the tribe. From the point of view of the political authorities he may often be obscurantist and obdurate. His main objectives are then to maximize individual not tribal gains. In the present times, with such vast development schemes afoot, the malik may well ignore sectional or tribal benefits to better his bargaining position vis-a-vis the political authorities. He may actually oppose (directly or indirectly) the construction of a road or school in his village. He has two reasons for doing so. The first, and obvious one, is the expectation of monetary or other rewards. The second is more subtle. He feels that with any change in the status quo of the village, whether in the educational or economic spheres, there comes a corresponding change in his social position and political hegemony. Sons of junior brothers or cousins may be more hard-working or more clever than his own sons. The balance in his section of tribal society is tilted with changes and, though not necessarily, against him. So while he may talk of wanting change he fears its long-term consequences.

The variety of maliks is confusing and ranges from actual tribal leaders with real patriarchal authority to those who do not even live in the Tribal Areas and have no influence among their section. Their numbers grow in a geometric proportion that would have alarmed Malthus. There are the 'hereditary' maliks, the 'recognized' maliks, (i.e. recognized by Government), the 'unrecognized' maliks (in cases 'self-appointed'), the *spin giray* (*white beards*), the *lungi-holders* and the *inam khors* (literally *eater of rewards*); the last two may not even be tribal maliks but merely enjoy the rewards of political favour bestowed by some Political Agent on their ancestors. If we were to divide the entire tribal population by the total number of recognized maliks (leaving the unrecognized ones alone for the nonce) we would see that one malik roughly represents no more than about a hundred people. These figures clearly show that he certainly does not speak for his entire tribe, as he might often wish to claim. In fact the average malik is a demographic representative of a typical three-generation tribal joint family of between eighty and a hundred people. It is the rare malik who towers over the section. A real leader of the entire tribe is even more rare.

The maliks whether 'hereditary', *lungi-holders* or *inam khors*, thus form a sort of basic democratic organization and represent its worst aspects – their number, in contrast to the population they are supposed to represent, clearly underlines the above comparison and the system's inherent flaws.

Today the tribesman is acutely aware that with the promise of democracy in the Settled Areas he is still subject to an anachronistic system whereby his so-called tribal representatives rarely visit their own agencies and areas. It is an open secret that most of the Afridi and Mohmand maliks living in Peshawar seldom visit their areas. The maliks in turn perpetuate their role as 'brokers' between government and their clans by acting as a barrier between the two. As mentioned above, all development schemes invariably have to come to terms with the maliks by diverting a certain percentage of their funds to them. Adult franchise, one of the major demands of the vociferous *kashars*, would not only reveal their socio-political impotence but finally erase them as a pressure group, as it is known today, from the Tribal Areas.

Mians and mullahs have traditionally been the subject of a bad press by writers on the Frontier. This was natural in the context of an imperial, British and Christian administration. Today the mians and mullahs can be, and have been, successfully used to further governmental efforts. The mians and mullahs ought to be understood in terms of the genealogical charter which excludes them from any inherent rights except by external association. The traditional outlook can be stood on its head in respect of this group. Experience has shown their willingness to risk life and property to help government. For instance various religious leaders helped persuade the Mohmands to accept the road successfully in 1974. Even the heir to the famous Faqir of Ipi, Niaz Ali, in North Waziristan has been of assistance to the political authorities. The mullah has lost his main argument and platform in representing his tribe against government because government is no longer foreign nor of a different religion. The traditional role of the mians and the mullahs has been to act as a buffer between tribes and subtribes and as intermediaries when the tribes clash among themselves. His everyday role is rather humdrum and only concerned with *rites de passage* (birth, circumcision, marriage and death ceremonies). He is in no way a pretender for tribal leadership unless in times of extraordinary crisis or political upheaval. He does not feature in the tribal genealogy and does not participate in the tribal *jirga*. He is acutely aware of his technical 'outside' status in the tribal structure.

There are a number of semi-humorous stories about him and his role in tribal society. Perhaps the classic story, although apocryphal, in this regard is that of the mullah who went into Afridi Tirah and berated the tribes for not having a single shrine or holy tomb. The Afridi answer was to kill the mullah and set up his shrine as the first religious one in the area.

Therefore, while they might be a reactionary force in the villages of the other provinces in the Tribal Areas the mullah and mian may be enlisted as agents of change. They often speak Urdu and are familiar with the current trends in the country. The mian and the mullah would want change because through these new sources of economic and social mobility can they hope to rise in the tribal structure. A good example is provided by Mian Mandi, the only market for the entire Mohmand tribe and Agency. As the name signifies it is owned and managed by the mians. The mians in turn use their influence in ensuring the Mandi area as a sort of neutral zone where shooting and brawling are disallowed. It is popularly believed that no shot fired in the Mandi area will find its mark and this belief is supported by various recent anecdotes.

EMERGING GROUPS:
STUDENTS AND CONTRACTORS

The students are not yet a fully-fledged pressure group except in the headquarters of the old agencies which house colleges, as in Miran Shah and Parachinar. For instance, the newer agencies like Mohmand, Bajaur and Orakzai do not face this problem (the last has no college yet). However, their contacts and studies in the Settled Areas and the growing general consciousness of the rights of the common man will make them an important pressure group in the coming years.

Politically a more important and refractory emerging pressure group is that of the contractor and dealer. These are the product of various forces, many 'developmental', and even the peculiarity of the 'permit' system which allows 'permits' for essential commodities, like sugar, to certain representatives of the tribe. They often manipulate a situation to the detriment of law and order. They have local knowledge and now have the money even to organize armed 'action groups' such as the *Chalweshtis* in Miran Shah or Wana. This group will continue to emerge, in direct proportion to the decline in authority of the traditional groups, and may be able to turn a situation to its advantage when faced with a vacillating administration. However, both the above groups, if properly handled need not pose a problem or challenge to the political authorities. They see and appreciate the winds of change and are therefore responsive to governmental endeavours and its policies of socialization; today, the contractor comes forward with positive and constructive suggestions for the better utilization of funds available or better distribution of rations. Whatever else they might be, they are the product of this era and therefore keen to continue the pace of social and economic change.

8

Education as a factor of socio-political change

Of all the development activities perhaps the one with the most far-reaching effects on social life is in the sphere of education. It is also here that perhaps the most sensational results have been achieved. For example, in 1956 the state of education may be gauged from the fact that there were only three graduates from the South Waziristan Agency (Mian, 1956, p. 31). Today there are literally hundreds and Mahsuds contribute to the development of the nation at all levels of Government: today a Political Agent is a Mahsud and so is the Additional Chief Secretary of the Province. The tribal sees senior government officials from his own area or tribe and this whets his appetite to understand and be part of the system that permits the attainment of such office and reward. For instance, today three Political Agents out of seven are tribals.

Perhaps nothing better illustrates the intense spirit ·of competition and the quality of the tribal boy than the Peshawar University Honours lists of 1975. Two coveted Presidential Awards and three Gold Medals for coming first in a subject were won by tribal boys. One of them, from North Waziristan, won both the Presidential Award and the Gold Medal by topping the M.B.B.S. examination. So far this honour and place in medicine have been the preserve of boys from the Settled Areas. A boy from South Waziristan balanced his northern cousin's achievements by topping the list in the Master of Arts examination and winning a Gold Medal. These prizes also indicate future trends. The tribal is no longer content to sit in the fastness of his mountains and let the world pass him by. He is coming down into the arena of the Settled Areas with its vastly superior facilities to participate, compete and, as these examples show so well, win.

The following table shows the increase in the total number of schools, High, Middle and Primary, since 1956.

NUMBER OF HIGH, MIDDLE AND PRIMARY SCHOOLS

Agency	1956	1971	1976
1. Bajaur	—	28	139
2. Mohmand	31	28	128
3. Khyber	22	45	140
4. Orakzai	—	26	136
5. Kurram	54	77	147
6. North Waziristan	53	66	150
7. South Waziristan	55	100	226
Total:	215	370	1,066

The totals reveal that within the short space of four years the number of schools increased almost *three-fold* between 1971 and 1976 and almost *five-fold* between 1956 and 1976.

Enrolment of students in all three categories of schools showed a similar sharp rise:

	1971/2	1975/6
Primary	44,385	82,946
Middle	6,012	12,339
High	1,730	6,045

The total number of students in schools recorded a *two-fold* increase over this period from 52,127 in 1971/2 to 101,330 in 1975/6.

Together with the increase in student numbers, the annual scholarships and grants for tribal students have *trebled* over the last four years as the figures (page 55) indicate.

Scholarships sanctioned increased almost *three-fold* between 1971/2 and 1975/6.

These students and schools are now producing the sort of person who will grow up within the larger socio-cultural context of Pakistan, who will want a

A Hindu and a Sikh of Orakzai Tirah

A visit by Mr. Z. A. Bhutto, Prime Minister, to Kalaya, Orakzai Agency

Primary school for girls (Orakzai Agency)

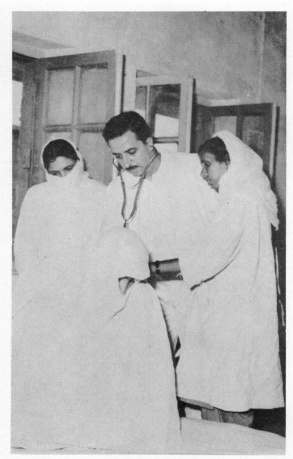

Hospital, Miranshah (North Waziristan)

SCHOLARSHIPS SANCTIONED   (in rupees)

Agencies	1971/2		1975/6
1. Bajaur	191,400	('73)	300,000
2. Mohmand	118,906		620,000
3. Khyber	58,200		87,200
4. Orakzai	130,000	('73)	268,000
5. Kurram	125,008		459,000
6. North Waziristan	188,100		364,000
7. South Waziristan	212,880		565,000
Frontier Regions			
8. Peshawar F.R.	12,040		31,200
9. Kohat F.R.	6,000		8,800
10. Bannu F.R.	65,200		313,000
11. D. I. Khan F.R.	13,650		2,3400
Total	1,121,384		3,139,600

better and different quality of life and whose horizons are neither limited nor blighted.

Now that this tremendous physical achievement has been recorded a reassessment of the direction of education is under way. The emphasis may reasonably shift from building new schools to building future citizens. The emphasis may also shift from producing generalist students studying for the B.A. or M.A. to those learning technical skills for various crafts demanded by the growing ·technical needs of the country.

9

The road as symbol of socio-economic development

Of all development activity the road is surely the most vital. It is not only a symbol of economic penetration but also one of socio-political penetration. All Political Officers agree that the road is like a needle that pricks the balloon of tribal superstition, foreign propaganda and economic backwardness. The major roads have been the key to the control of the trans-Indus area— and indeed the key to the gateways to the sub-continent: the major routes into South Asia from Central Asia lie here. From earliest times the passes here have been used: Alexander marched through the Nawa Pass (shared between the Mohmand and Bajaur Agencies and located on the Durand Line). Tribal roads were built over the last hundred years as much a result of 'push' by the British seeking military advantage as 'pull' by local minority groups. For example, the Wana Wazirs, the Kurram Shia and the Orakzai Shia invited the presence of the established government to 'protect' them from ethnic or sectarian majorities.

The major achievement has been the opening of new roads and the reopening of old disused roads over the last couple of years. The change of heart is striking: in 1973/4 almost every yard of the Yousaf Khel – Nawagai road through the hitherto inaccessible Safi area had to be negotiated. Today the Safis themselves want the benefits the road has brought: schools, dispensaries, electricity. One of the most critical and early break-throughs, both from an economic and strategic point of view, was the opening of the Yousaf Khel – Nawagai road through virgin Safi territory.

Similarly the road building activity in Orakzai and Kurram Agencies will penetrate into hitherto inaccessible Afridi Tirah. The Kurram road has already reached the Afridi Tirah border (fifteen and a half miles from Sadda) and the Kalaya road in Orakzai Agency has gone up to Kalat, two miles beyond Kalaya itself. The reoccupation of old forts such as those at Datta Khel, Razmak, Ladha and Tiarza ensure the continuing use, improvement and protection of the connecting roads. A notable setback has been the Tirah road in the Khyber Agency; this, however, is a temporary setback and not a permanent failure. It is significant that the psychology of the Tirah Afridi is already changing with the now busable Kalaya road. Scores of Afridis, of all ages and sexes, cross over daily into Orakzai Agency and pay the six rupee fare to be taken from Kada to Kohat town, from where they can take a bus to anywhere in the country. Their argument now remains purely 'political' and it is only a matter of time before the Afridis themselves want their own road out of Tirah. Expenditure on roads increased from one million rupees in 1971 2 to 61.9 million rupees in 1975/6. As well as a barometer of economic activity, the road serves a strategic purpose: for the first time in Pakistan's history the nation's most inaccessible borders (along the Durand Line) are guarded and manned.

MAJOR ROAD-BUILDING PROJECTS

Agency	Route	Distance (miles)
Bajaur	1. Construction of Munda–Khar–Nawagai black-top road	30
	2. Inayat Killa–Ghakhai Pass road	11
Mohmand	1. Construction of Yousaf-Khel–Nawagai road	28
	2. Construction of road from Yousaf-Khel–Nawagai road to the most convenient point leading to the Nawa Pass on the Afghan border	12

Khyber		Construction of Landi Kotal (Inzari Fort)–Loe Shilman road	15
Orakzai	1.	Improvement and construction of Kacha-Pakka–Kalaya road (Suleman Khel Road)	38
	2.	Construction of Marai–Daulatzai road	26
Kurram		Sadda–Dogar–Zera Mela road	15½
North Waziristan	1.	Re-opening and improvements of Miran Shah–Datta Khel road	26
	2.	Re-making of Thall–Spin Wam–Mir Ali road	36
	3.	Dossali–Gariom road	13½
South Waziristan		Re-opening of Razmak–Ladha–Tiarza–Wana road	48

One apparent consequence of the new roads is the great impetus to move in vehicles. In many cases, as for instance medical emergencies, reaching a road can save a life if the patient can be transported in time to hospital. In other cases, too, the social habits of a thousand years are rapidly dying. I have seen Safi tribesmen, who would normally walk south from Lakaro (in the north of the Mohmand Agency and recently come to life because of the road) over the Nahakki Pass to Mian Mandi or Ekkagund, refuse to take a step until the bus arrives. When it does there is a scramble for seats and passengers will happily cling onto the body of the bus or sit on the roof rather than walk. Today, after the first service began in 1974, there are almost a dozen services between Lakaro and Mian Mandi.

The road-building activity and its scale has generated auxiliary economic activity. One of the concessions Government makes in this regard is that contracts are, by and large, awarded to tribal contractors. Another clause is that labour employed should be local (usually provided from the tribal section through which the road is passing). This ensures new employment opportunities to the tribesman in his own area.

With the opening of the roads has come a host of related developments such as electricity, which has gone beyond Lakaro (mentioned above) and almost reached Nawagai. Electricity to the Loe Shilman area in the Khyber Agency was switched on in August 1976 and electricity poles already stand along the major Orakzai road up to and even beyond Kalaya, the future agency headquarters, in Tirah. In North Waziristan it has reached Razmak. In South Waziristan it is at Jandola and electricity poles are being put up to take it to Wana. It is hoped to make connections to Wana and Kalaya within this year. Electricity brings with it the economic laws of 'increasing returns': tube-wells and irrigation schemes are possible which in turn mean more general prosperity and better standards of living.

10

New economic opportunities

The intentions of both the central and provincial governments in their efforts to develop the Tribal Areas may be gauged by the total size of the Annual Development Program. The following figures indicate the expenditure in the Tribal Areas (they include the expenditure of the Federally Administered Tribal Areas Development Corporation but exclude certain schemes such as the building of hostels and Central Road Schemes):

	Rupees (000*s*)
1970/1	8,043
1971/2	16,994
1972/3	23,948
1973/4	78,307
1974/5	201,476
1975/6	231,287
1976/7	246,050

As can be seen from the figures, expenditure in the Tribal Areas has increased *thirty-fold* in the last four years. This increase is notably greater than the proportionate increase in the Annual Development Program over the same period for the Settled Areas and makes a striking picture on the graph:

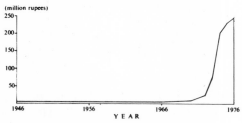

Allocation for power and electrification schemes increased more than *twenty-fold:*

1971/2	0.41 million rupees
1975/6	11.64 million rupees

The 'electrification of Waziristan' project alone will cost almost 42 million rupees.

Health projects that include hospitals and dispensaries also received full attention as can be seen from the expenditure figures below:

1971/2	0.174 million rupees
1972/3	0.02 million rupees
1975/6	12.56 million rupees

As a result there has been an overall increase in the following medical facilities:

	1971/2	*1975/6*
hospitals	32	39
dispensaries	99	128
rural health centres	1	3
maternity/child centres	9	9

Today there is a total bed strength of 1511.

In the sphere of public health engineering, the increase in expenditure is equally remarkable:

1971/2	1.5 million rupees
1975/6	10.4 million rupees

Similarly, the housing sector shows remarkable progress:

1971/2	no provision
1975/6	12.3 million rupees

The above figures include the new civil colonies at Khar, Nawagai, Ghalanai, Miran Shah and Razmak.

The expenditure on agriculture shows a similar increase:

		Total crop acreage
1971/2	1.3 million rupees	89,000 acres
1975/6	12.5 million rupees	150,000 acres (1974/5)

During the last four years an area of nearly 10,000 acres has been reclaimed/developed and 1.9 lakh fruit plants raised and distributed. Three sericulture centres, each training twenty people annually, have been opened at Kalaya, Parachinar and Miran Shah.

Similar increases were made in the animal husbandry sector:

1971/2	0.4 million rupees
1975/6	3.2 million rupees

and in the Forestry Department:

1971/2	0.2 million rupees
1975/6	1.8 million rupees

Expenditure on the Peoples Works Programme and the Integrated Rural Development Programmes increased from a virtual zero in 1971 to 7.5 million rupees this year, involving 269 schemes. The first IRDP centre was selected and opened in the Tribal Areas this year at Parachinar, Kurram Agency.

The cost of the new schemes included in the fifth Five Year Plan (1976-81) total 1,246 million rupees distributed as follows:

	Rupees (million)
Water sector	313
Industrial sector	923
Mineral sector	11
Total	1,247

The Federally Administered Tribal Areas Development Corporation, an agency established exclusively for the Tribal Areas, has been rapidly taking on larger developmental commitments with every passing year:

	Budget allocation (*Rupees million*)	Expenditure (*Rupees million*)
1970/1	0.2	0.1
1971/2	4.0	3.9
1972/3	15.8	9.4
1973/4	25.1	28.0
1974/5	58.0	57.7
1975/6	61.7	45.0*

Within its short life its budget allocations have increased from under 2 lakh rupees in its first year, 1970/1 to 617.16 lakhs in 1975/6.

---

* This expenditure is up to June 1976.

Among the major Federally Administered Tribal Areas Development Corporation achievements, some complete and some well on the way to completion by the end of the year, and spread equitably over the Tribal Areas, are:

Agency	Project	Cost (*Rupees million*)
Mohmand	Glass factory (will employ about 150 people)	2.5
Khyber	1. Bara River Canals Scheme (will irrigate 49,312 new acres) —completed.	52.3
	2. Bara Cigarette manufacturing factory producing 30 million cigarettes annually—completed	8.1
	3. Bara Vegetable Ghee Mill (will employ 150 people)—completed	19.8
Kurram	1. Shalozan Irrigation Scheme (will irrigate 3,500 new acres)	3.2
	2. Zeran Irrigation Scheme (will irrigate 2,000 new acres)—completed	4.0
	3. Fruit and Vegetable processing plant (will process 1,500 tons of fruit and vegetable annually and employ 38 people)	6.0
North Waziristan	1. Match factory at Miran Shah (employs 100 people)—completed	11.0
	2. Carpet yarn making factory at Miran Shah (will employ 40 people)	7.0
	3. Idak and Khajuri tube-well irrigation scheme (will irrigate 4,000 new acres)—6 tube-wells commissioned	1.0
South Waziristan	1. Footwear and leather goods factory at Spinkai Raghzai (will employ 210 people)	9.8
	2. Leather tannery at Spinkai Raghzai (will employ 120 people)	9.6
	3. Spin Plain Irrigation Scheme (will irrigate 10,000 new acres)	6.2

Wheat, sugar and rice, much needed commodities in the rest of the country, were generously diverted to the Tribal Areas over this period as the diagram below shows and increased in quantity *two-fold:*

Agency	1972			1975/6 (in tons)		
	Wheat	*Sugar*	*Rice*	*Wheat*	*Sugar*	*Rice*
Bajaur	1,581	—	—	1,644	—	—
Mohmand	5,500	955	20	18,192	1,944	40
Khyber	8,610	1,173	20	17,796	1,653	40
Orakzai	4,693	1,974	—	7,818	—	20
Kurram	3,000	727	20	10,920	1,388	20
North Waziristan	3,910	584	20	8,460	1,023	20
South Waziristan	2,600	842	20	7,240	1,252	20
Total	29,894	4,281	100	72,070	7,260	160

An additional allocation of one lakh tons of wheat has been made for the Federally Administered Tribal Areas during the current year above the existing quota.

Therefore the Tribal Areas are today using 172,070 tons of wheat 7,260 tons of sugar and 160 tons of rice annually as compared to 29,894 tons of wheat 4,281 tons of sugar and 100 tons of rice in 1972.

It is significant that whereas in 1971 the team of experts appointed to investigate and prepare an industrial investment schedule for the Tribal Areas could not visit three of the then five Political Agencies (CATADC Year Book 1971/2, p. 37) today no area is out of bounds or inaccessible for such activities.

Such large injections of money through such schemes obviously have both a general economic 'spill-over' effect and also activate the principle of the economic 'multiplier' effect. These projects are thus creating centres of employment and economic betterment.

With the extension of the banking laws, the Tribal Areas may soon see the next phase which is in the offing: private enterprise in the industrial field. The limits are unbounded as these areas are rich in mineral wealth: cement, marble, precious and semi-precious stones and other minerals such as chromite and copper.

Finally, as old forts and posts are reactivated in the older Agencies (Dossali, Datta Khel, Razmak, Gariom, Ghulam Khan in North Waziristan and Sararogha, Tiarza, Ladha in South Waziristan) and new civil quarters constructed in the newer agencies (Ghalanai in Mohmand, at Nawagai and Khar in Bajaur and soon by the Mastura river opposite Kalaya in Orakzai) further 'spill-over' economic effects are becoming apparent: employment, transport and better standards of living.

Miranshah College (North Waziristan)

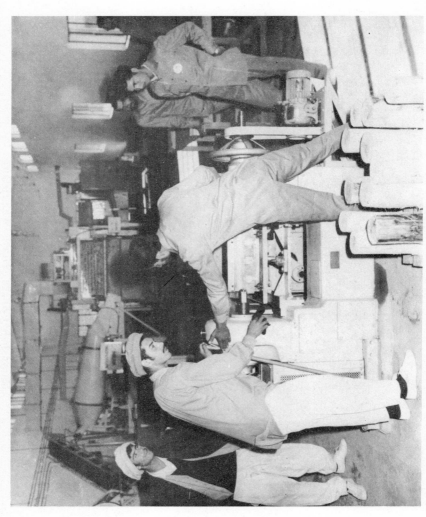

Match factory, Miranshah (North Waziristan)

11

Conlcusion: consolidation
of development

The Prime Minister's visits have irrevocably changed the formal nature of *jirgas* and public assemblies. His example and the precedent could be used to invite religious divines such as the Imams of Mecca Sharif and Madina Sharif who toured Pakistan recently. The tribesman is a staunch Muslim and this would open the window onto the larger Islamic world and, in turn, into the Tribal Areas. These assemblies should be open to one and all and need not be held in the headquarters but in the actual centres of population, however remote.

If planned according to the sensitivities of local ethnic and sectarian configurations the visits of international Islamic divines could make a terrific socio-religious impact. For example, Shiah religious divines from (say) Iran could visit Shia areas in Kurram or Orakzai Agencies, or Islamic (Arab) scholars could visit Lakaro (Mohmand Agency), for example, possibly to participate in a seminar on the life of the Haji of Turangzai (who spent so much of his life fighting the British from there early this century).

An unprecedented event took place when a representative all-tribal *jirga* of thirty-five maliks (five from each agency) was invited to the airport ceremonies at Islamabad to receive King Khaled of Saudi Arabia on his State visit to Pakistan in October 1976. The impact on the tribesmen, who are deeply aware of the status in the Islamic world of the keeper of the greatest places of reverence, the twin cities of Mecca Sharif and Madina Sharif, can be imagined.

Tourists, especially from Pakistan, should be encouraged to visit the agencies, especially the older more 'settled' ones like Kurram. New tourist arrangements at Kalaya, would attract many tourists keen to spend a night in the famous Tirah itself. This will act as a two-way process in integration as well as generate local economic uplift, it will also remove the veil of mystery that hangs on the Tribal Areas.

Sikhs and Hindus live peacefully within the tribal structure in such remote places as Kada, Orakzai Tirah. They talk and dress like the tribes that have given them land and protection. Their actual daily existence and harmonious social life could well serve as an example both for the country and abroad: non-Muslim groups are living in perfect harmony in the most remote spots of the Tribal Areas—lands famed for their religious *jihads*, beliefs, and, as this fact surely proves, tolerance.

POLITICAL OFFICERS

Good officers are desirable for every form of government duty and in every place. In the Tribal Areas the Political Agent, forming the apex of the administrative pyramid, still wields far greater influence and power than his counterpart, the Deputy Commissioner. To the tribesmen he is government. Political Agents must therefore be, as they have been in the past, selected from the cream of the services.

The rapid emergence of the tribal peoples poses a new and relevant question: ought local tribes to be administered by their own tribal officer? In theory this may sound feasible but in practice this could be disasterous, for example, a Dawar in North Waziristan, a Shia Turi in Kurram or a Mahsud in South Waziristan would create or exacerbate certain problems inherent in the local conflict and ethnic patterns. It is suggested that Tribal Areas be considered 'specialized areas' but that tribals in service be considered fit for posting anywhere in Pakistan and not in their native agencies.

As officers who serve in the Tribal Areas invariably undergo certain hardships and require a missionary attitude to work two essential elements must be introduced in their postings. The first is some form of material incentive. Although this may be considered incompatible with a missionary spirit it may help assuage the feelings of relatives or wives anxious to remain in large urban centres. The second is consultation with the officers of their willingness to go for periods of two to three years. Too often officers, either in the Scouts, or even doctors or teachers, look on postings in the remote areas as a form of *kala pani* (literally *black waters* – any remote, uncivilized place is so called). This attitude is neither helpful to their organization nor to the people they serve.

CO-OPERATIVE SOCIETIES

Co-operative societies are said to have generally failed in the Settled Areas and the rest of Pakistan but for the government now looking around for tribal institutions to act as receptacles for its various developmental activities they may provide a viable answer, as each joint family or extended family represents a unity of social and economic purpose unmixed by other tribal or class groups. If the Co-operative Societies Act is extended to the Tribal Areas the tribal structure could quite conveniently provide ready made socio-economic institutions for such development activities as the provision of credit facilities, seed procurement, marketing and irrigation schemes.

Sooner or later the problem of involving women in the larger developmental framework will have to be considered. No people's effort can ignore women. Co-operative societies alone could provide the only possible means of involving women in the developmental effort. Women co-operative officers could supervise women's societies in providing credit for handicraft and knitting etc.

CONSOLIDATION

The tribesmen's religious affiliation with the rest of the country cannot be doubted (for example the spontaneity and fervour with which the Mohmands, Afridis, Wazirs and the Mahsuds participated in the troubles in Kashmir 1947/8) nor their economic propensities: D. I. Khan, Bannu, Kohat and Peshawar provide the main markets for the adjoining tribes. Over the last few decades, and especially since the formation of Pakistan, the tribesmen have been descending at a rapid rate into the Settled Areas. Almost half the Mohmand population is said to be in Mardan and Peshawar Districts. The Afridis are in and around Peshawar in large numbers and the Orakzais are in and around Hangu. The Wazirs are in Bannu and the Mahsuds almost control Tank in D. I. Khan district. As a writer who spent a lifetime in the Frontier Province summed up 'The Pathan future is not in doubt; it lies, as it has always lain, with the people of the Indus Valley.' (Caroe, 1965, p. 437).

Today there are more Pathans living in the Punjab and Sind Provinces than in the Tribal Areas. Karachi is the biggest Pathan city in the world (with over a million and half). It is time now to by-pass the vested interests in the Tribal Areas who would want to continue discrimination and segregation for their own limited benefits. The tribesman is not and cannot be a Red Indian. But the restless energy and surge of humanity that has been recently tapped can only be given a meaningful expression within the fabric of Pakistan. The tribesman is a Pakistani in every sense of the word and will continue to participate in the growth processes of the nation in the most meaningful manner possible. This fact is essential in understanding his socio-psychological problems and needs. The great development effort of the last few years, both in physical achievements and psychological break-through, must now be consolidated. We must ask certain questions, time and history will provide their answers or show their validity.

Bara Dam (Khyber Agency)

In conclusion, we may recapitulate the main strands in the argument:

The past tendency of the traditional political authorities was to spread a curtain of ignorance and mystery over the Tribal Areas. This curtain is now in the process of being removed. Traditional political thinking is aptly described in this passage: 'Here (on the Frontier) the tribes were still treated like tigers in a national park. They could kill what deer they liked in the park; they risked a bullet if they came outside and took the village cattle.' (Woodruff, 1965, p. 291). Today, the tiger moves freely throughout the country. He is no longer the predatory beast pictured in the reference above. He is just another Pakistani going about his business in an endeavour to earn a livelihood or better his lot. He is a tamed tiger.

We have seen that traditional tribal Pathan focus and interest were centred around two forms of leadership—the saintly and the chiefly. Today a third viable form, in both a political and a non-political sense, is the emergence of the common or average tribesman.

The battle for the future of the Tribal Areas is neither political nor ethnic but largely economic and it will be decided on this front. Today the winds of change that are blowing in Pakistan also blow in the most remote ravines, gulleys and valleys of the Tribal Areas. Nothing can be the same again. Tribal social and economic structures are so deeply inter-related that changes in one will trigger changes with far-reaching ramifications in the other. Extensive economic and social development programmes can prepare us for deep structural changes in tribal society—changes especially dramatic as they are the first on this scale and style in over a thousand years.

Bibliography

Ahmad, S (1973) 'Peasant Classes in Pakistan' in *Imperialism and Revolution in South Asia* (ed. K. Gough and H.P. Sharma), Monthly Review Press.

Ahmed, A.S. (1976) *Millennium and charisma among Pathans: a critical essay in social anthropology*, Routledge and Kegan Paul, London.

Alavi, H. (1971) 'Politics of Dependence: a village in West Punjab'. South Asian Review, January.

Asad, T. (1970) *The Kababish Arabs*, Hurst and Co., London.

    (*ed.*) (1973) *Anthropology and the Colonial Encounter*, Ithaca, London.

Bailey, F.G. (1960) *Tribe, Caste and Nation*, Manchester University Press.

    (1961) 'Tribe and Caste in India' in Contributions to Indian Sociology, October.

Barth, F. (1953) 'Principles of social organization in Southern Kurdistan', Universitets Etnografiske Museum Bulletin, Vol 7, Oslo.

    (1959a) *Political leadership among Swat Pathans*, LSE monograph, Athlone Press, London.

    (1959b) 'Segmentary opposition and the theory of Games', JRAI London 89 pt 1.

    (1961) *Nomads of South Persia*, Allen and Unwin, London.

    (1970) *Ethnic groups and boundaries: the social organization of culture differences*, Allen and Unwin, London.

Bruce, R. I. (1900) *The Forward Policy and its Results*, Longman, Green & Co., London.

Burnes, A. (1961) *Cabool*, Ferozsons, Lahore.

Caroe, O. (1965) *The Pathans*, Macmillan, London.

Churchill, W.S. (1972) *Frontiers and Wars*, Penguin Books, Harmondsworth.

Dube, S.C. (1965) *Indian village*, Routledge and Kegan Paul, London.

Edwardes, H. (1963) *A year on the Punjab Frontier* (Vols. I and II), Ferozsons, Lahore.

Elphinstone, M. (1972) *An Account of the Kingdom of Caubul*, (Vols. I and II), Oxford University Press, Karachi.

Evans-Pritchard, E. E. (1949) *The Sanusi of Cyrenaica*, Oxford University Press, London.

Fortes, M. and Evans-Pritchard, E.E. (*eds*) (1970) *African Political Systems*, Oxford University Press, London.

Fraser-Tytler, W.K. (1967), *Afghanistan*, Oxford University Press, London.

Fuchs, S. (1974) *The Aboriginal tribes of India*, Macmillan, Delhi.

Fox, R. (1967) *Kinship and marriage*, Penguin Books, Harmondsworth.

Gellner, E. (1969) *The Saints of the Atlas*, Weidenfeld and Nicolson, London.

Gluckman, M. (1971) *Politics, Law and Ritual in Tribal Society*, Basil Blackwell, Oxford.

Hailey, Lord (1957) African Survey, London.

Inayatullah and Shafi (1964) *Dynamics of development in a Pakistani village*, PARD, Peshawar.

King, W. (1900) *Monograph on the Orakzai country and clans*, Punjab Government Press, Lahore.

Kipling, R. (1960) *Kim*, Macmillan and Co., London.

Leach, E. (1940) *Social and economic organization of the Rowanduz Kurds*, LSE, London.

Lewis, I.M. (1969) Conformity and Contrast in Somali Islam in *Islam in Tropical Africa*, Oxford University Press, London.

Lewis, O. (1958) *Village life in Northern India*,

Lyall, A. (1882) *Asiatic Studies: Religious and Social*, London.

Maine, H. (1861) *Ancient Law*, London.
    (1871) *Village Communities in the East and the West*, London.

Masters, J. (1956) *The Lotus and the Wind*, Penguin Books, Harmondsworth.
    (1965) *Bugles and a Tiger*, A Four Square Book, London.

Mayer, A.C. (1970) *Caste and Kinship in Central India*, Routledge and Kegan Paul, London.

Mian, N. I. (1956) *Economic Survey of Tribal Areas*, Board of Economic Enquiry, Peshawar.

Middleton, J. and Tait, D. (*eds*) (1970) *Tribes without Rulers* Routledge and Kegan Paul, London.

Nadel, S. (1942) *A Black Byzantium*, London.
    (1947) *The Nuba*, London.

Peters, E. (1960) 'The proliferation of segments in the lineage of the Bedouin of Cyrenaica'. Vol 90 pp 26-53 JRAI, London.

Pettigrew, H.R.C. *Frontier Scouts*, Selsey Press, Sussex, England.

Population Census 1972 (1975) *Federally Administered Tribal Areas*, Interior Division, Islamabad.

Spain, J. (1963) *The Pathan Borderland*, Mouton, The Hague.
    (1972) *The Way of the Pathans*, Oxford University Press, Karachi.

Swinson, A. (1967) *North-West Frontier*, Hutchinson and Co., London.

Tapper R (1971) 'The Shahsavan of Azarbaijan' Ph.d. thesis, London University (SOAS).

Toynbee, A. (1961) *Between Oxus and Jumna*, Oxford University Press, London.

Warburton, R (1900) *Eighteen Years in the Khyber,* John Murray, London.

Woodruff, P. (1963) *The men who ruled India*, Vol. II *The Guardians*, Jonathan Cape, London.

Year Book (1971-72) Centrally Administered Tribal Areas Development Corporation, Peshawar.

Index